UNDERSTAND[ING]
THE ROCK AR[T]
OF SEDONA
AND THE VERDE VALLEY

Kenneth J. Zoll

VERDE VALLEY
ARCHAEOLOGY
CENTER

ISBN-13: 978-0-9820378-4-3

Library of Congress Control Number: 2008907399

Published by VVAC Press
Verde Valley Archaeology Center, Inc.
385 S. Main St., Camp Verde, Arizona 86322
www.verdevalleyarchaeology.org

All photos by the author
Cover image: V Bar V Heritage Site
Previous page image: Red Tank Draw
Back cover image: Near Palatki Heritage Site

CONTENTS

PREFACE

The Verde Valley hosts a unique and varied representation of prehistoric cultural sites. It is the host to two National Park Service National Monuments, three U.S. Forest Service Heritage Sites, five protected sites owned by the Archaeological Conservancy, the Yavapai-Apache Nation, and over 2,500 archaeological sites. The mission of the Verde Valley Archaeology Center is to preserve archaeological sites and collections and to promote their educational, scientific and cultural use. We advocate for the preservation of the Verde Valley's irreplaceable cultural resources that include significant structures, sites and artifacts. Through education and information, we provide leadership to the regional community on the critical issues of understanding and preserving our rich cultural heritage.

The Center is dedicated to enhancing the knowledge of the prehistory and ethnology of inhabitants of the Verde Valley region. We promote a greater understanding of the diversity of cultures, past and present, for our guests and the citizens of the Verde Valley. We advocate for the retention and preservation of the Verde Valley's irreplaceable cultural resources that include significant structures, sites and artifacts.

There are over 450 recorded rock art sites in the Sedona/Verde Valley area. Many visitors express great interest in the rock art at the cultural heritage sites. The docents receive many questions about these images. Who made them? How have they lasted this long? What do they mean? This book is not a scientific monograph on rock art. It does not contain elaborate bibliographic sources, although some are quoted and referenced. This book is intended to be a useful and thought-provoking introduction to the vast, scattered and sometimes unpublished literature on rock art, with specific focus on images and styles found in the Sedona/Verde Valley area. It is hoped that it will promote reflection on and appreciation of the people who created the rock art.

ACKNOWLEDGEMENTS

This book, or my knowledge of rock art for that matter, would not have been possible without the opportunity that Friends of the Forest provides as part of their Cultural Resources Committee and the Verde Valley Chapter of the Arizona Archaeological Society activities. In addition, the patient docent training sessions by Coconino National Forest Archaeologist Peter J. Pilles, Jr. has benefitted the entire Sedona area through the knowledge he has passed on and the heightened sense of our cultural preservation needs.

I would like to thank Al Cornell for providing the bulk of the information on how pictograph pigments were made. Thanks to Ekkehart Malotki, professor of languages at Northern Arizona University, for his draft review and helpful suggestions. Thanks to Frieda A. Eswonia of the Yavapai-Apache Nation for historical tribal information. Thanks also to Chris Coder, archaeologist for the Yavapai-Apache Nation for his review and counsel on the material related to the Nation's rich history in the Verde Valley, as well as for the use of the Yavapai territorial map. I also appreciated the editorial comments and suggestions by Travis Bone, archaeologist for the Forest Service Red Rock District. And thanks goes to Dr. William Green, Director of the Logan Museum of Anthropology at Beloit College for use of the map of prehistoric cultures of the Southwest from their excellent website.

WHAT IS ROCK ART?

INTRODUCTION

Rock art is a term commonly used for the designs and other intentional markings that people made on natural geological surfaces. Rock art occurs across the United States but the greatest concentrations are found in four regions:

- California
- The Great Basin of Nevada and western Utah
- The Columbia Plateau of Washington, Oregon and Idaho
- The Southwest which includes Arizona, New Mexico, eastern Utah, southwestern Colorado and western Texas.

Though a widely accepted term, some believe that it is a misleading term in that it has not been established that all rock art images were items of "personal expression" as the term "art" is used today. The term "rock writing" has been used by others, but this implies that it is a system of symbols, such as hieroglyphics, which is incorrect. To try to convey a more accurate meaning, rock art is sometimes referred to as cultural markings, or rock markings. Although cultural marking is probably a better term, the popular term remains rock art.

Another term that is sometimes used is ***rupestrian art***. This is the term given to graphical and sculptural works that pre-industrial man has left on hillsides, scattered rocks and the walls of cave and grottos. Their origins may go back as far as 30,000 years, to the beginning of the upper Paleolithic era.

Of course after we settle on what to call these images the ultimate question that every visitor asks is – "What does it mean?" Unfortunately, that answer will never be straight-forward. In fact, some argue their meaning is unknowable. It is true that we cannot apply our Western traditional systems of symbolism and thought to understand what the rock art meant to people hundreds of years ago. These people were of a different time, of a different culture, with different religious beliefs, and different survival needs.

There are no ancestors alive today in the American Southwest who lived within the pueblo cultures and can tell us exactly what the creator of these ancient images meant to convey. However, the inhabitants of the ancient cliff dwellings who abandoned those locations long ago did not simply vanish. They moved on for various reasons and adopted different methods to survive in the arid Southwest. There are descendants of many of these peoples alive today. For example, it is generally acknowledged among archaeologists that the Hopi and Zuni are descendants of the ancient pueblo people such as the Anasazi (currently referred to as the Ancestral Puebloans), Sinagua, and possibly the Mogollon. Likewise, the Pima and Papago (now referred to as Tohono O'odham) tribes in the Phoenix/Tucson areas are regarded as the descendants of the Hohokam. But even these generalizations ignore the complexity of prehistoric population movements, e.g., the Hopi clans that are Hohokam.

It must also be accepted that historic Pueblo societies have been participants in the evolving traditions of their Southwestern cultures from the time of the prehistoric Pueblos. It would be unsupportable to contend that innovations and modifications were not made by historic cultures as the rituals and practices were passed along. Interaction among villages, different cultures, as well as the rise of new leaders and ceremonial concepts, would be expected to bring change and the diffusion of the original intent.

So much has changed over the centuries for the current descendants, not the least of which was the arrival of the Spanish in the 1580s and the missionaries during the ensuing centuries. Because of these influences and the melding of cultural traditions through inter-marriage, interpretations of prehistoric rock art by these current cultures are equally questionable. In fact, interpretations of the same image can vary within the same culture and even within the same village. While treated with respect, without an archaeological trail (ethnographic record) to the "ancient ones," such interpretations are suspect.

So, are we to view rock art with frustration, never to know their meanings? The short answer is "sometimes." There are a number of images that currently defy interpretation. However, rock art research efforts undertaken over the last twenty years or so have contributed significantly to understanding prehistoric social and religious development and organization. Likewise, correlations have been made between rock art images and those painted on later ceramics and kiva (ceremonial room) walls.

Some believe that rock art, of any type, should never be interpreted since no direct descendants remain and only someone of that culture could understand their intent. Other rock art scholars disagree and suggest that some sense can be made of the images through careful study and research.

New dating techniques have also shed light on the images. In some cases, items on a single panel that had previously been thought to have been created during the same time period have been shown, through these new dating techniques, to cover different time periods. Direct dating methods have also shown that previous interpretations are sometimes wrong. As dating techniques and new discoveries are made, the interpretation of rock art images will undoubtedly be revised.

The material contained in this book reflects some of the current research and thinking on the rock art of the Sedona/Verde Valley area. Any such interpretive effort necessarily starts by understanding the different types of rock art.

PETROGLYPH
(Greek: petro = rock; glyph = carving)

Petroglyphs are pecked, ground or scratched into a rock surface. All are created by removing a portion of the rock's surface. They often remove the natural rock coating, or rock varnish (described in detail later), to reveal the natural rock colors beneath.

How are petroglyphs dated?

There is no absolute method available at present to date petroglyphs. Attempts to date petroglyphs through indirect methods use the following techniques:

Figure 1.1 Petroglyph pecked into sandstone bluff

Style — The style of the rock art can establish date ranges associated with the culture that created it. For example, knowing the rock art styles of the people who inhabited the Verde Valley over the centuries can provide a chronological framework to apply to a rock art image.

Linking to artifacts — If the petroglyph can be associated with other materials, with reliable dates, found in proximity to the rock, its age can be inferred.

Superimposed designs — Often petroglyphs are superimposed over one another. Such superimposed designs can provide a relative age.

Repatination — The rock varnish, through which people created the petroglyphs, will begin to recover the glyphs. The color can at least be used to compare relative ages among the petroglyphs.

Figure 1.2 Petroglyph of exquisite detail

Absolute Dating – The methods described above are all referred to as relative dating. Relative dating techniques try to determine which rock art images are older and which are younger in some particular setting. On the other hand absolute, or scientific, dating is a way to get the exact date of something in the most accurate way possible, such as tree-ring dating or radiocarbon dating. Unfortunately, there are no generally acceptable absolute dating techniques that can be applied to petroglyphs. While some attempt has been made to date the organic rock varnish inside petroglyphs, conditions vary so widely that this has proven to be a tantalizing but allusive tool.

PICTOGRAPH
(Latin: picto = paint; graph = write)

Pictographs are paintings or drawings made on rock. They were done in one or more colors. Pictographs were easier to make than petroglyphs so they tend to contain more complex features. However pictographs are also more fragile. The ones that have survived are in protected areas such as underneath rock overhangs as found at the Palatki and Honanki Heritage sites.

How are pictographs dated?

The dating of pictographs is similar to those methods used to date a petroglyph:

Style — Identifying the style can establish date ranges associated with the culture that created the image.

Linking to artifacts — If the pictograph can be associated with other material with reliable dates, the rock-art age can be inferred.

Superimposed designs — Often pictographs are superimposed over one another. Such superimposed designs can provide a relative age.

Radiocarbon dating — Accelerator Mass Spectrometry Radiocarbon (AMS) dating is a scientific technique used for pictographs. A small portion of organic material is removed for testing. The only organic pigment is charcoal. The other colors, such as red and white, are from minerals. However, organic substances can also occur in the binders (described in the next chapter) used to make the pigment, which could be extracted and dated through AMS.

Radiocarbon dating has been used on the pictographs in the Sedona area. One study was performed at Palatki/Red Cliffs in 1999 on the geometric forms shown on the next page. This image has several components. There is a large black form with white dots and human-like figures at the top. One of the white dots in the black form was radiocarbon dated to A.D. 1600 (± 100 years). The group of humans at the top was radiocarbon dated to A.D. 1180. To the left of this image are two round shield-like images (shown later on page 47). The shield on the left is highly eroded compared to the shield on the right. Black pigment in the left shield was removed and radiocarbon dated to A.D. 700 (± 100 years).

Figure 1.3 Palatki Heritage Site pictograph on which radiocarbon dating was used.

So what does this dating information tell us? If the geometric form and the shield-like images were created at about the same time, then it tells us that the white dots were added later. But for what purpose? As we will see, rock art interpretation is difficult and sometimes impossible, even with sophisticated dating techniques.

CUPULES

A unique, and often overlooked, type of rock art is referred to as *cupules*. These are generally regarded as among the oldest forms of rock art. Cupules are small, bowl-shaped shallow depressions. They are pounded, pecked or ground into rock surfaces. Sometimes the depressions also show evidence of grooves. These are then referred to as "pit and groove" style cupule petroglyphs.

Cupules are found all over the world. In the United States, they occur most frequently west of the Rocky Mountains. California has numerous cupule sites, as does the western portion of the Great Basin. In Southern Arizona, cupules have been documented at Rillito Peak, the

Figure 1.4 Multiple cupules on boulder. More are on the other side.

Picacho Mountains and numerous sites in the Coronado and Tonto national forests. In Northern Arizona, they are found in the Little Colorado River Basin and at numerous sites in the "Arizona Strip" (from I-40 north to the Arizona-Utah border). Here in the Sedona/Verde Valley area they are found at Palatki-Red Cliffs, the V Bar V and along Bell Trail, among other locations.

It is possible that some circular depressions on horizontal surfaces were used for some utilitarian process such as grinding food, pigments or other material. However, there are distinct differences between cupules and grinding hollows or bedrock mortars. Grinding hollows are formed by abrasion (rubbing one rock against another). They occur only on near-horizontal surfaces and are often large, with slopping side, with evidence of grinding. True cupules, on the other hand, are found on vertical walls and boulders, and are relatively small.

Why were cupules made?

Cupules rarely occur singly. They usually form groups, sometimes numbering in the hundreds on a single panel or boulder. Cupules tend to be arranged systematically, for instance in rows or multiple rows, while at other locations they appear to have been done randomly. A wide range of purposes of cupules has been suggested.

In the few cases where ethnographic meanings have been secured for cupules in North America, east Africa and Australia, it is suggested that the function was often, though certainly not always, ceremonial or symbolic. In California, the Plains, and the Northwest Coast, cupules are part of women's puberty, birth, and fertility rites. In some California locations they are referred to as "thunder rocks," used in a rain-calling ceremony to produce ritual thunder by striking the cupules. A number of sites in southern California connect cupules to astronomical events.

Little is recorded in pueblo ethnography to account for cupules in rock art. It is very doubtful that all cupules were made for similar purposes. In Northern Arizona, some cupules have been suggested to have a boundary marking purpose. The Hopi have been recorded performing a healing practice of visiting the room of an ill person and grinding a cupule-like depression in the wall of the pueblo. The depression is then filled with "prayer (corn) meal" and the appropriate prayer feather is inserted into the mixture.

In New Mexico, the Zuni have a ritual of visiting a sacred boulder said to be covered with cupules regarded as "female fertility symbols." To aid a woman's fertility or to ensure the gender of a future child, a cupule is ground into the boulder and a drink is made of the resulting dust. This practice is referred to as *geophagy* which is defined as the practice of eating earthy substances such as clay or rock powder. This practice is not confined to Native American cultures. In Germany, cupules on churches were thought to possess healing qualities. Patients are reported to have swallowed the powder produced in grinding out the cupules. Those with fevers then blew their sickness into the cupule. There is also a report that describes two stones in France attached to churches where people ground holes in the stones and drank the powder to cure fever and impotency.

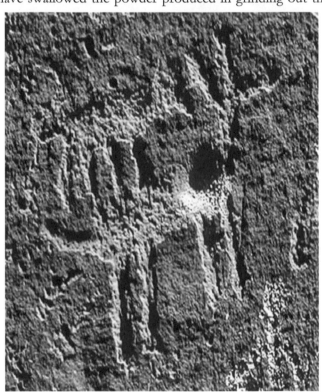

At the V Bar V Heritage site, there are 69 petroglyphs containing cupules. The cupules are found in the figure's head and/or heart. While most of the figures are zoomorphs, there are a few within anthropomorphs. This is the largest concentration of petroglyphs containing cupules anywhere in the Verde Valley. Because of the quantity of cupule images, it is believed that this was a significant ceremonial area. However, it is not certain whether the cupules were made at the time the figures were created or were added later.

Since cupules are found infrequently in the Sedona area, they will not be described further. However, they can be seen at several locations in the Verde Valley that are identified in the chapter on visiting sites.

Figure 1.5 Cupule in the heart area of this animal figure

GEOGLYPH
(Greek: geo = earth; glyph = carving)

Geoglyphs are drawings or designs produced on the ground sometimes called intaglios. Geoglyphs made by arranging stones, stone fragments, gravel or earth create a positive geoglyph. These are also sometimes called a rock alignment. Geoglyphs made by removing the outer surface of the ground (similar to desert varnish) to expose a lighter color ground surface produce a negative geoglyph, sometimes referred to as a petroform.

Some of the most famous negative geoglyphs are those found in Peru. These are of such a large scale that they can only be fully appreciated by flying over them. Geoglyphs are also found in Australia and parts of the Great Basin Desert in Utah. There are also geoglyphs in Arizona. One of the better known is the "Blythe Intaglios" on Bureau of Land Management property near Blythe, Arizona. There are a total of six figures in three locations. A human figure is found at each site, while an animal figure is present at two locations. The largest human figure measures 171 feet (52m) from head to toe.

There is only one known geoglyph in the Verde Valley of Arizona. It is a rock alignment in a snake-like shape. It is at the top of a 3,400 foot (1,036m) mesa near Sinagua ruins and other interesting archaeological features that are still under study. It is made of arranged stones stretching about 85 feet (26m) in length, undulating in a north-south direction. It averages 3 feet (1m) in height and the width varies between 3 and 4 feet (1-1.2m). At the "head" of the formation there is an opening as though simulating an open mouth. The function of this alignment has been suggested to be a solar calendar. A gap in the center of the alignment is opposite a series of uprighted rocks to the east that combine to produce distinctive shafts of light and shadow at the equinox and solstices.

Figure 1.6 The only know geoglyph in the Verde Valley forms a snake-like image.

2
HOW WAS ROCK ART MADE?

The techniques used by prehistoric and historic cultures to produce rock art were varied. This section will examine these techniques in some detail, dealing specifically with those techniques used in the Sedona/Verde Valley area.

PETROGLYPHS

Petroglyphs are found on the dark, exposed surfaces of rock such as sandstone and basalt. These surfaces serve as the base color for the images. The rock surfaces are often covered with rock varnish, described below. There are several techniques for making petroglyphs:

- Striking the base rock directly on the surface with another rock is called ***direct percussion***. The edges of petroglyphs created with direct percussion are often jagged.

Figure 2.1 Petroglyph by direct percussion

- Fine details are achieved with ***indirect percussion***. Indirect percussion refers to pecking the surface of a rock by holding a pointed tool as if it were a chisel and striking that with a hammer stone to peck evenly-sized, closely-spaced, circular dents. Often the material between the dents is removed with a scraping tool. Greater control was achieved using this method.

Figure 2.2 Petroglyph by indirect percussion

- Images are sometimes made through **abrasion** of the rock surface in a back-and-forth rubbing motion. These images do not display significant detail.

Figure 2.3 Petroglyph by abrasion

- Some rock art is **scratched** into the rock face. These fine lines are often difficult to see unless the lighting is at the right angle. In prehistoric times, a lithic flake or blade was probably used.

Figure 2.4 Petroglyph by scratching

WHAT IS ROCK VARNISH?

Many petroglyphs are found on rocks or surfaces covered with rock or desert varnish. Rock varnish is one of the most remarkable biogeochemical phenomena in arid desert regions of the world. Although it may be only a hundredth of a millimeter in thickness, rock varnish often colors entire desert mountain ranges black or reddish brown. Rock varnish is a thin coating (patina) of manganese, iron and clays on the surface of sunbaked boulders and cliff walls. Rock varnish is formed by colonies of microscopic bacteria living on the rock surface for thousands of years. The bacteria absorb trace amounts of manganese and iron from the atmosphere and precipitate it as a black layer of manganese oxide or reddish iron oxide on the rock surfaces. This thin layer also includes cemented clay particles that help to shield the bacteria against desiccation, extreme heat and intense solar radiation.

Varnish bacteria thrive on smooth rock surfaces in arid climates. Thousands of years are required for a complete varnish coating to form in the deserts of the southwestern United States. The chemical process by which the desert varnish is formed is called **patination**. In fact, the degree of patination, or rather the **repatination** of an image, is sometimes a useful tool for the relative dating of varnished surfaces. This can be of enormous importance to the study of desert landforms and to the study of early humans in America, since many artifacts lying on the ground become coated with rock varnish.

On occasion, the interior of petroglyph images will appear to have been painted with various shades of green. While there is evidence that some petroglyphs were filled-in with paint, the green seen on, around and within rock art is most likely *lichen*. Structurally, lichens are among the most bizarre of all forms of life. That's because every lichen species is actually composed of two other distinct species of organisms. One species is a kind of fungus, and one is a species of algae. Lichens are a symbiotic association of a fungus and an alga.

The removal of lichen from rock art is not an option. The processes employed by the lichen have already "softened" or destroyed the underlying petroglyphs. Removing the lichen would not "restore" it and, in fact, may produce greater damage.

PICTOGRAPHS

Pictographs are usually found on light-colored, protected surfaces. Pictographs were considerably more complex to make than petroglyphs because of the materials required for

Figure 2.5 Typical rock-varnished surface with lichen

paint. The predominant colors are red, black, white and yellow. Blue and blue-green are rare and depend on available local pigment sources. Differences in shades come from varied composition of the minerals in different areas. It was not the custom to blend colors. Clay was the best source for mineral pigments. Plant pigments were rarely used because they tend to fade rapidly.

1. Red/Red-Brown is the oldest pigment. The sources of this color were:

   - Red ochre
   - Iron oxides: Hematite – looks black; Hualapai hematite is prized as the best in the West, even today. Limonite was also used.

Figure. 2.6 Pictograph with red pigment

2. Black was produced from charcoal, or soot.

Figure 2.7 Pictograph with black pigment

3. White was produced from several sources. The clays of the mineral pigments are often off-white, but they brighten with heat.

- Kaolin clay (hydrous aluminum silicate)
- Gypsum and selenite
- Soapstone (talcum steatite)
- Chalk
- Ash
- Bone, shell

Figure 2.8 Pictograph with white pigment

4. Yellow is rare but was produced from:

- Iron oxide
- Pollens, e.g., cattails
- Red barberry root w/kaolin clay

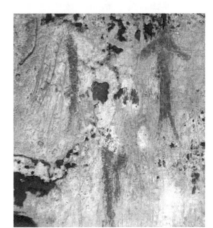

Figure 2.9 Pictograph with yellow pigment

5. Blue-green is likewise rare. It was achieved from:

- Malachite
- Azurite (found in the Jerome area)
- Turquoise (powdered residue from making jewelry, carvings, etc.)

Figure 2.10 Pictograph with blue-green (faded) and white pigments

These pigments had to be mined or obtained through trade. As a rule, once obtained, they were ground, and then mixed with water. The liquid would then be drawn off without disturbing the fine pigment sediment. Any remaining solution would be left to dry, leaving a fine powder film. After several repetitions using new ground material, there would be a layer of fine pigment powder in the bottom of the drying vessel. The technique is called **settling**.

Red pigment was stored and transported in cakes formed of pigment and animal blood. Any pigments might be stored in tightly closed leather pouches or cariso tubes (also called **fragmites**, a reed which is found in the Verde Valley).

The dried pigments would be transported to the rock art site and then blended with a binding agent to make it fluid for painting. Among the probable binders were the following:

- Yucca juice – very good, clear. They would roast the leaf until rubbery, and then squeeze juice out by pressing across it with the flat of a knife or stone.
- Animal fat – deer and bear are most common. It was rendered so that it would not go rancid. Bear fat stays liquid at room temperature, so it was easy to use. Animal fats mute the colors slightly.
- Hide glue – After first cleaning and before curing, they would scrape the hide well, boil the scrapings for a long time and then strain the lumps out. The resulting mixture hardens for easy transport. It is then reconstituted with water when needed.
- Egg yolks, whites
- Saliva, blood, urine
- Sap – some evergreen saps are very clear.

The rock would sometimes be abraded to smooth the rough spots. This extends the life of the painting by improving the bond. A small pool of a binder and some pigment powder were put in separate places on a flat rock. The brush would be wet in the binder, and then the pigment was touched, mixed and painted. By using this method instead of premixing, none of the valuable pigment was wasted. Ideally, a fine pigment and the binder form a strong bond with the object, even to the molecular level.

The paints would be applied in a variety of ways. Applicators included:

- Fingers or hands
- Brushes of fur, hair, fiber, moss or feathers
- Twigs (chewed), yucca leaves (softened by pounding the end, then stripping outer cover with a blade)
- Charcoal or mineral pencils

3
WHO MADE THE ROCK ART?

EARLIEST INHABITANTS

Most archaeologists agree that the first inhabitants of the Americas came to the new world by way of the Bering land bridge, when the strait between Siberia and Alaska was dry land. However, intense controversy remains over exactly when this occurred. One school of thought suggests that the Americas were colonized as early as 40,000 BC. A second hypothesis argues that the first crossing occurred perhaps about 18,000 years ago, during the late Ice Age. Some also argue that settlement took hold after the Ice Age, as recently as 13,000 BC.

Arrival of the paleo-indian cultures in the Sedona/Verde Valley area has been estimated at about 11,500 BC. These paleo-indians were the hunters of large mammals (megafauna) such as mastodons, wholly mammoths, saber-toothed cats, bison, shrub oxen, camels and giant sloths that ranged over wide areas. The presence of megafauna in savanna-like areas of the Verde Valley suggests that paleo-people must have found the area attractive.

Only recently has there been evidence that proves the existence of paleo-people in the Verde Valley. The first Clovis projectile point in the area was found at Honanki about 1995. These distinctive projectile points were first discovered near Clovis, New Mexico, which gives these points their name. This culture appears to have traveled extensively, following the big game. Four other Clovis points have been found in the Sedona/Verde Valley area since 1995. All the projectile points were found in the uplands area of the Valley, probably because the lower parts of the valley have filled in with alluvial soils. Most of the Clovis points are made with local materials such as fossil sponge and fine-grain basalt; although one point was hardscrabble dacite, which is local to the Payson area. That projectile point was found at Crescent Moon Ranch, indicating trade or movement within a fairly large range. Clovis points are known to have been used for hunting large animals, including elephants, which inhabited the Verde Valley at that time.

For reasons still unclear, all megafauna became extinct by about 9,000 BC. While scientists agree that something dramatic happened 12,000 years ago to cause the relatively sudden loss of the megafauna, evidence of that "something" remains elusive. Absent a meteor crater, one theory holds that a meteorite or comet entered Earth's atmosphere and disintegrated before exploding in a cluster of airbursts. These airbursts could have triggered a series of dramatic climate shifts including colder temperatures and an abrupt change in vegetation. This period is also referred to as the post-Ice Age Younger Dryas, or Big Freeze, that snapped Earth back to near glacial conditions for about 1,200 years. This change would have made survival difficult for large mammals. The big game hunters would have had to resort to hunting smaller game, not requiring the larger Clovis-style projectile points. Thus, these points "disappear" at the same time as the megafauna.

So the debate goes on as what caused the extinction of megafauna, the "collapse" of the Clovis big game hunter culture and the Big Freeze. What we do know is that the people who then roamed the Verde Valley after the extinction of the big game are called *Archaic* hunter-gatherers. We have long known that archaic people used this area from 2,000 to 6,000 years ago (the earliest date is another area of debate), until about AD 300. They were the Verde Valley's longest occupation group.

While these people continued to rely on wild game, they had an increased dependence on plant resources. They had semi-sedentary settlement patterns with seasonal migrations for plant and game. There is evidence of the beginning of experimentation with planting due to the abundance of plant food processing artifacts such as manos and metates.

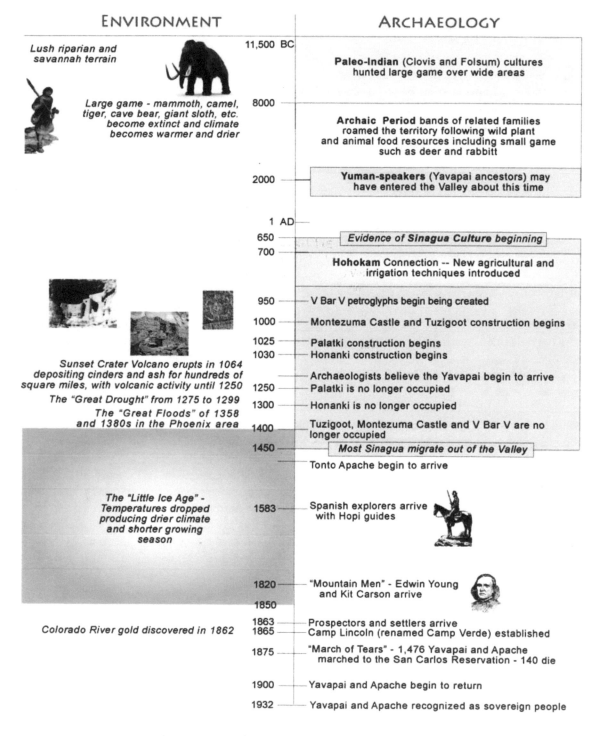

Figure 3.1 Timeline of environmental factors and inhabitant development in the Sedona/Verde Valley

EARLY ARCHAIC DESIGNS

No rock art has been found in the area that can be associated with the paleo-indians. However we begin to see rock art in the Sedona area with the emergence of the Archaic cultures. These markings have been covered by the natural processes to make them difficult to see unless the light is at the correct angle. This process, described earlier, is called **patination**. Many panels have been abraded or polished before being marked, a common Archaic characteristic. **Superpositioning** and patination help to differentiate early and later time periods.

Archaic grids, asterisks, etc., may be impressions of shamanistic visions. The shamanistic aspect of rock art comes into play for healing and when the spirits are communicated with during a trance at a site of power. If these represent the visions of the shaman during a trance, it would explain why the early and later images are so similar since these visions seem to be universal. They may have been made for use in interpreting visions. Other possibilities are to document that a particular ceremony was done here, or to document what was seen during that ceremony. Another possible explanation is that they are teaching tools for training younger tribal members. Hunter-gatherers made such geometric markings, as did some early agricultural cultures.

Red blob style (Western Archaic)

This style is normally associated with the period 6,000 – 650 BC but may be as late as AD 40 in the Verde Valley. Sometimes these large stylized human-like images are a purplish red. Often, these cover incised lines and are very faded due to aging.

Western Archaic

This style often includes lines of dotes, zigzags, squiggles, rakes, grids and were done late in the Archaic period in many colors. Late Archaic period runs from 3,000 BC to AD 100.

Figure 3.2 Early archaic scratched designs

Figure 3.3 "Red Blob" archaic style

Figure 3.4 Western archaic style

SINAGUA

The beginning of agriculture marked the end of the Archaic Period. About A.D. 650, a people who archaeologists refer to as the ***Sinagua*** made their presence known in the Flagstaff and Verde Valley regions. Sinagua is a Spanish term meaning "without water." There is debate as to whether these people came from east-central Arizona or developed in place from earlier archaic people. Some archaeologists consider these people to be a branch of the Mogollon culture who occupied eastern Arizona and western New Mexico.

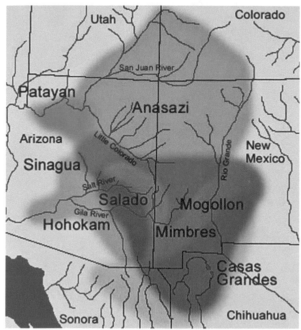

Figure 3.5 Southwest Prehistoric Cultures courtesy of the Logan Museum of Anthropology, Beloit College

Other archaeologists believe the Sinagua to be an independent regional culture that was affected by the Hohokam to the south, the Ancestral Puebloans to the north and the Mogollon to the east.

Archaeologists divide the Sinagua into two branches. The Northern Sinagua occupied the area around what is now Flagstaff, while the Southern Sinagua lived along the middle stretches of the Verde River. The Southern Sinagua quickly learned about the plants, animals, soils and climate of the Verde Valley and developed a dynamic culture. The rich mineral resources of the Verde Valley, and its central location between the Hohokam to the south and the Kayenta Anasazi to the north, resulted in active trade and an exchange of ideas that enriched all three cultures. After about A.D. 1125, archaeologists note widespread changes in southern Sinagua settlement patterns, architecture and ceramics. The Southern Sinagua expanded their occupation of the Verde Valley from primarily lowland areas to upland zones, foothills, cliffs and mesa tops. Various architectural forms proliferated from pithouses to small room blocks and, for the first time, constructed cliff dwellings in the Red Rock canyons around present-day Sedona. Ceramic production also changed to items resembling their northern neighbors with decreasing Hohokam traits.

This expansion was probably made possible by a slightly moister climate. A moister climate meant more consistent harvests. Irrigation canal networks were an important part of their agricultural techniques, as were elaborate systems of dry and floodwater-farmed fields. In the red rock canyons the Sinagua could raise their crops with dry farming techniques.

Between A.D. 1150 and 1300, the Southern Sinagua reached their maximum territorial extent, with villages of 3 to 10 families scattered throughout every niche in the Verde Valley. After A.D. 1300, the southern Sinagua began to move into a series of large dwellings, often on hilltops and other prominent points. The southern Sinagua congregated into about 50 pueblos - large masonry towns - each occupied by 20 to 100 or more families. Most of the pueblos were spaced along the Verde River and its perennially flowing feeder creeks, such as Wet Beaver Creek, linking the abundant wild plant and animal food resources of the uplands along the Mogollon Rim with the fertile farming soils of the Valley bottomlands.

This movement may have been precipitated by climate changes. Between A.D. 1300 and 1400, the climate fluctuated between wet and dry periods. Like other areas of Northern Arizona, the Verde Valley was generally abandoned by the Sinagua about A.D. 1400. By no later than A.D. 1450, the Verde Valley was abandoned to the extent that the southern Sinagua cultural pattern no longer existed.

The reasons for the abandonment are still unknown. Theories of drought, soil depletion, disease, warfare, invasion, and the dissolution of trade networks have all been offered. None seem to provide an adequate explanation alone. Most likely, it was a combination of several causes that came together at this time.

Dr. Brian Fagan in his book *The Great Warming*, points out that great

Figure 3.6 Sinagua pictographs

droughts, as experience in the late 13th Century of Arizona, would have tested ancient strategies of agriculture and trading. Ancestral Puebloans mastered this difficult environment through flexible and opportunistic movement (migrations). He holds that the "pattern of movement was a familiar strategy in an area where rainfall ebbed and flowed and no single community was completely self-sufficient."

The ultimate fate of the Sinagua is unknown though it appears that many migrated to the east and then to the north near Winslow, Arizona for a time, eventually finding their way to the Hopi mesas, Zuni and perhaps other pueblos in New Mexico. Some may have moved to the south to contribute to changes occurring in the Hohokam country.

There is significant evidence linking the Sinagua with the Hopi of historical times. There are Hopi stories of ancestral migrations from "the red canyons" to the southwest.

In addition, some archaeologists hold that not all the Sinagua left the

Figure 3.7 Sinagua petroglyphs

Verde Valley. It is believed that some may have remained and intermarried with the newly arrived Yavapai who then adopted the hunter-gatherer subsistence strategy of the Yavapai.

Besides the cliff dwellings, field houses and irrigation systems, the material legacy of the southern Sinagua can be found in their rock art. The Sinagua created both petroglyphs (direct and indirect percussion techniques) and pictographs (painted with even, strong and well-defined brush strokes of the entire color palette).

THE YAVAPAI AND APACHE

Yavapai and Apache history in the Verde Valley spans several hundred years, as two distinct indigenous groups that co-existed in surrounding areas.

The **Yavapai** are a *Yuman* speaking tribe, as are all Pai tribes (Hualapai, Havasupai, Yavapai, Pai Pai). Many archaeologists believe that they arrived in the Verde Valley around AD 1300, although their history suggests a much earlier arrival. They are linguistically unrelated to the Apache, who live in western and central Arizona. Due to the general similarities of material culture and subsistence adaptations, the Yavapai were often mistakenly referred to as "Apache" by Euro-American observers.

The Yavapai were semi-nomadic hunter-gathers who lived and travelled in small groups within specific home territories. The *Wipukupaya* group occupied the red rock country including Oak Creek Canyon and the area east to the Verde Valley.

The term **Apache** applies to a diverse group of Na-Diné (*Athapaskan*) speaking tribes and bands, who entered the Southwest before the arrival of Europeans. In the 19th century the Apaches inhabited a broad area from central Arizona to southern Texas and northern Mexico. Many Apache groups were nomadic or semi-nomadic and traveled over large areas, including areas visited or inhabited by other tribes. This makes it difficult to correlate geographic locations with any single specific cultural group, or even with a particular tribe. The Tonto-Apache arrived in the Verde Valley around 1450. Evidence of Tonto Apache (known to themselves as *Dilzhee'*, translated as "The Hunters") use is found in the Beaver Creek area, though some rock art at Honanki and Palatki indicates they were on the west side of the Sedona area as well.

When the Spanish explorer Antonio Espejo arrived in the Verde Valley in1583, he described the Yavapai and Apache as "rustic people" who "gave us what they had." They were described as a hunting and gathering people. The American entrance into Yavapai and Apache traditions began in 1860. Exploring and trapping parties had made their way here earlier, but no effort had been made to settle. In 1863, mining camps were established resulting in Indian hostilities that would continue without interruption until General Cook rounded up the surviving Yavapai and Apache and took them to the Rio Verde Reservation in 1873. This is referred to as the "conquest" by the Yavapai-Apache.

Figure 3.8 Yavapai pictographs

They remained there until March 1875, when an estimated 1,500 Yavapai and Apache were moved from the Rio Verde Indian Reserve 180 miles away to the Indian Agency at San Carlos. The forced removal, now known as Exodus Day, of the indigenous people of the Verde Valley resulted in several hundred lives lost and the loss of several thousand acres of treaty lands promised to the Yavapai-Apache by the United States government. When finally released, only about 200 Yavapai and Apache actually made it back to their homeland in the Verde Valley.

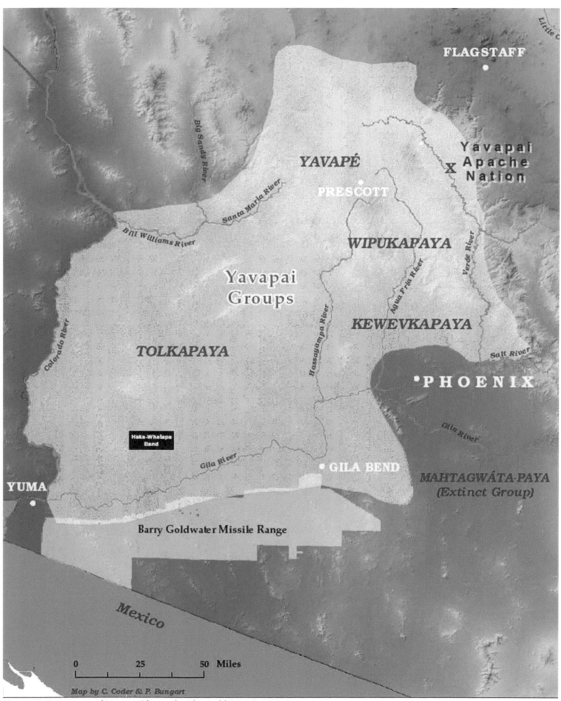

Figure 3.9 Ancestral Yavapai homelands and historic range

The modern Yavapai-Apache Nation is the artificial amalgamation of these two distinct cultures, who occupied opposite sides of the Verde Valley for centuries prior to the Euro-American conquest of the Southwest. The Nation as we know it today is the result of legislation passed by the Congress in 1934 known as the Indian Reorganization Act, in an effort to establish a single tribe in the Upper Verde Valley. This was done as an expedient by the federal government who believed that the shared experience of the Yavapai and Apache at San Carlos from 1875 to around 1899 rationalized this as a legitimate act. Today the several satellite communities of the Nation truly reflect the evolution from two historically distinct Tribes into the single Nation of today. The Nation is a single political entity, but still respects its dual heritage as an important legacy for all of the descendants from those times. The reservation today spans 665 acres in the four communities of Camp Verde, Middle Verde, Clarkdale and Rimrock.

Yavapai and Apache rock art was produced by scratching or painting. Pictographs were produced in black (charcoal) and red (ochre) and commonly mixed with mescal syrup, other plant juices and deer fat. The paint was applied with the fingers or small sticks.

Since the Apache are relatively recent arrivals to Arizona in the 1500's, many images portray historic images such as horse-and-rider. Other typical Apache images are animals, wavy lines, lizards and masks.

Yavapai rock art styles include scratched and pecked petroglyphs. Few Yavapai painted images appear technically identical to Sinagua pictographs, although the subject matter is often the same. A particularly distinctive Yavapai method is called the mud paint style (or stucco style). These images are often in red-orange or white. The paint is thick and mud-like. They are several millimeters thick and quite fragile, often partly *spalling* from the rock surface.

Figure 3.10 Yavapai petroglyphs

4
WHAT IS IT?

Attempting to interpret a rock art image is a risky business. The primary problem is that we would need to understand the cultural context in which the maker of the image was living at the time. For example, in today's popular culture if someone is described as being "hot" or "cool" it is unlikely that they are referring to their internal body temperature. If we even go back to Shakespeare, when the playwright calls a person "cheap" he is not referring to his monetary tightness, but rather he is insulting the person with a term we would understand as "vulgar."

When visitors come to the cultural heritage sites in the Sedona/Verde Valley that have rock art, one of the very first questions asked is "what does it mean?" Visitors have a fascination, not just with the imagery, but with the purpose for which these ancient people made the images. Some believe that the rock art provides a window into ancient beliefs because the images are embedded into the landscape, or that the images are pictures of the experiences of these prehistoric people.

Archaeologists tell us that a great deal of rock art was made in the context of the spiritual world of the cultures that created the images, although some images were made to inscribe information about the physical world. Rock art, therefore, can tell us something about the ritual practices and social identity of the earlier cultures.

But rock art images are not a system of symbols like sign language or Egyptian hieroglyphics. This possibility has been carefully studied and discarded by rock art scholars. However, some Native Americans object to referring to ancestral rock art as "prehistoric" that is defined as the time before written records. Native Americans point to rock art as their form of written records.

Also unsupported is the thought that these were merely doodling or the graffiti of the day, with no cultural significance to the makers. While it would be presumptuous to think that no rock art was done to pass idle time or for fun, the vast majority of prehistoric rock art does not fit this simplistic interpretation.

There is also debate whether any of the rock art was intended as "art for art sake." Some argue that rock art was not done in the way the Western mind associates the term with "fine art" that is done for no function beyond the aesthetic. Others argue that every human being has had the proclivity to create pleasing images (that today is called "art"). To deny these ancient people this natural behavior is to deny them a part of their human nature. But, while not claiming any parallel, I find it interesting that today's modern art frequently needs an art critic or art specialist to tell us what a given piece of art "means."

In addition to asking "what is it" rock art specialists also ask "why was the image placed here?" This question is studied in the specialized fields of *landscape archaeology* and *archaeoacoustics*. Space does not permit a full discussion of these areas. Suffice to say that landscape archaeology explores the way cultures perceived and used the earth's surfaces for rock art, while archaeoacoustics studies the sound (echo) characteristics of rock art placement. For example, it has been observed that certain types of images appear more frequently along waterways. Likewise, very large rock art sites often have unusual acoustic properties that may have caused the site to be selected to enhance ceremonial chanting, singing and drumming.

Although individuals may offer interesting suggestions or interpretations of rock art images, the fact remains that they cannot be sure unless the interpretation can be generalized beyond the single case. Archaeology is a social science that relies on patterns of behavior, not isolated acts. Rock art analyses and interpretations must be based on empirical data gathered in a systematic manner to show that it is representative of the population of similar images.

While determining the exact meaning of a rock art image is difficult, many images can at least be placed within a *functional category*. This general approach, described below, begins by attempting to understand what we are looking at. This section will give you some of the more common terms used to classify rock art images, with examples of each.

ANTHROPOMORPH

An ***anthropomorph*** is an image that resembles a human figure.

Figure 4.1 Anthropomorph pictograph

Figure 4.2 Anthropomorph petroglyph

Zoomorph

A *zoomorph* is an image that resembles an animal. Animal-like images with four legs are often referred to as *quadrupeds*.

Figure 4.3 Zoomorph pictograph with anthropomorph figures

Figure 4.4 Zoomorph petroglyph

SNAKES

The prevalence of snake-like zoomorphs in the Verde Valley deserves some discussion. The depiction of snakes, or serpents, appears repeatedly in many southwestern cultures. Snakes are revered and used in rituals and ceremonies. They are often viewed as the messengers between humans and the underworld. This symbol goes back to at least A.D. 1000 in Pueblo cultures. Images of snakes are common in the Ancestral Puebloan (Anasazi) areas of Chaco Canyon in New Mexico, southeastern Colorado and east of the Rio Grande River.

Many believe that the origin of snake imagery began with ***Quetzalcoatl***. This plumed serpent — a snake with a plume of feathers above its head — image has its origins in the great city-states of southern Mexico, or Mesoamerica. Plumed serpent iconography is common in Mesoamerica. They represented regeneration of the life-giving energy of the earth because they shed their skins and are regenerated themselves. Moving between the upper world and the lower world, they were often symbols of the supernatural. Because of their fluid movements, they were also associated with moving water. Many of these symbolic references were carried forward into Southwestern cultures.

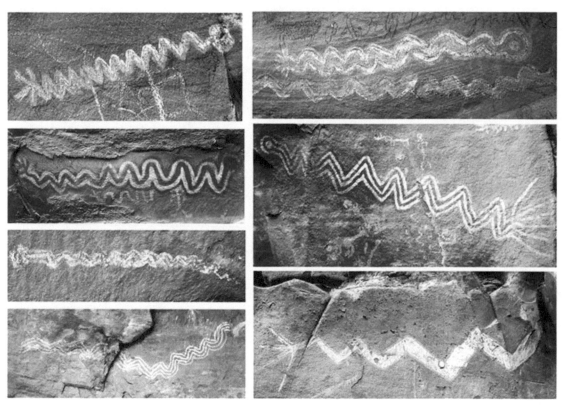

Figure 4.5 Mosaic of snake-like zoomorph pictographs

Brought north into the Southwest, possibly by traders, Quetzalcoatl is said to have given the people corn, domesticated animals, irrigation technology and fire. In some Pueblo societies, he commands underground water sources and is the guardian of pools, waterfalls and springs. Encountering a snake on the way back to a village from a spring is considered a good omen. However, if displeased, he can cause earthquakes and floods. In historic pueblos, the plumed serpent is known as Ko'lowisi at Zuni, Palulukong at Hopi and as Aywanu at the Rio Grande pueblos.

The Hopi respect the role of the snake in the balance of nature and venerate them as symbols of fertility and war. The plumed serpent plays a prominent role in their ceremonies at the Vernal Equinox and at the Winter Solstice. In some Pueblo fertility rituals, snakes appear as celestial serpents, or lightning symbols, that bring summer rain but also potentially destructive violence.

The Snake Dance is probably the most well-known of the Hopi ceremonies. Priests gather live snakes for use in the dance. The snakes are kept in pots while altars are made. It takes at least nine day to carry through all phases of the Snake Dance. On the last day of the ceremony, the snakes are taken out of the pots and bathed. After the snakes are dried, they are taken into the villages where dancers dance with the snakes in their mouths. Once the dance ritual is over, the priests sprinkle the snakes with corn meal and then release them. The Hopi believe that the snakes will return to the gods and report that they were treated well. The gods will then give the Hopi the rain they need for a good crop.

It is not surprising, therefore, that we find many Sinagua snake pictographs and petroglyphs in the Sedona/Verde Valley area.

Figure 4.6 Mosaic of snake-like zoomorph petroglyphs

FOOTPRINTS AND HANDPRINTS

Depictions of human footprints and handprints are commonly found throughout the Southwest. A *positive* handprints is one in which the hand is covered with paint and pressed against the rock surface. A *negative* handprint is one in which paint is sprayed around a hand placed on the rock surface leaving an outline form.

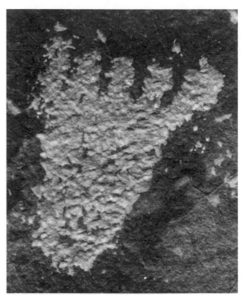

Figure 4.8 Footprint petroglyph

Figure 4.7 Positive handprint pictograph with anthropomorphs

Figure 4.9 Negative handprint pictograph

ABSTRACT ELEMENTS

Depictions of abstract elements are among the most difficult to understand and ascribe a meaning. They are also called *geometrics*. Geometric designs can be bounded (within a square, rectangle or circle), unbounded patterns, as well as single abstractions. Bounded motifs are composed as a unit of decorative features in a symmetrical or asymmetrical arrangement.

Images composed of single and complex groupings of lines, circles, dots and patterns may symbolize concepts familiar to the makers, or they may represent natural forms in very stylized ways. Patterns of repeated elements, without a central focus, are considered to be patterns typical of Sinagua textiles. Many woven fabrics, basketry and ceramic vessels are found with similar abstract motifs.

Figure 4.10 Geometric bounded motif pictograph

Figure 4.11 Repeated pattern abstract pictograph

Research has suggested that our brain (the visual cortex) finds geometric forms very pleasing. Perhaps this is why dots, short lines, rakes, zigzag lines, parallel lines, circles, grids, ladders, curvilinear, rectilinear and other forms are common, as was shown in the earlier Archaic images. However, since it is impossible to place these abstract elements in the original cultural context in which they were created, erroneous and incomplete interpretations are likely. For example, is the image in Figure 4.12 a basket design, a net, a farm field exhibiting the "waffle" effect of stone alignments, a type of game board, or the floor plan of a multi-room pueblo? The answer may be any of these or "none of the above."

Figure 4.12 Geometric pictograph

Figure 4.13 The meaning of this geometric petroglyph will probably never be known

While the image to the right at least provides a few possibilities, the image below is beyond our current understanding.

Another theory interprets some abstract geometric rock art as the work of shamans or medicine men that drew natural symbols brought to the mind's eye when in a trance. We find suggestions of this type of rock art primarily at the Palatki Heritage site. Large panels are covered with both apparent designs and random scratching said to represent an *entopic vision* while in a trance.

SHIELDS

A form of abstract design that appears to be more easily identifiable is that of a ***shield***. Shield-like images appear frequently in the Southwest. The shields are often decorated with various line and dot designs as are the shields of Honanki shown below. The shields at Palatki likewise have decorated features. Since these shields are found in association with habitation sites, it has been suggested that they may be a type of "family crest" for the family units living in that area, but that is not certain.

Figure 4.14 Shield pictographs at the Honanki Heritage Site

Figure 4.15 Shield pictographs at the Palatki Heritage Site

5
WHAT DOES IT MEAN?

Many purposes and meanings have been proposed for rock art. Images related to religious beliefs are the most prominent. From Archaic through historic pueblo periods, rock art seems to have been a way to communicate with the gods and supernatural forces. In doing so, rock art could become infused with supernatural powers. Some older rock art images are found to have been repecked or retouched by later people perhaps to take advantage of or regenerate these powers. Alternatively, some rock art is found to have been defaced or have evidence of attempts to remove them entirely. This may have been done as attempts to remove bad spirits or omens represented by the images. Some of this activity has been attributed to early Apache arrivals and therefore may reflect changing belief systems and interpretations of the images.

Rock art is often found near habitation sites and areas of human activity. It is sometimes suggested that some were done as a pastime. Although some images are crudely executed and apparently meaningless, these are clearly in the minority. The difficulty of making pictographs or petroglyphs may have deterred the casual maker. The scarcity of unskilled images, plus the placement and content of the imagery suggests a definite purpose and meaning.

Ethnography is the study of a group of living people – how they live and interact, what they believe in, what kinds of objects they use, and what they do. It focuses on one group at one place in time – ethnographers (sometimes called cultural anthropologists) generally live and interact with the people they are studying.

Ethnography is frequently used by archaeologists to understand materials from the past. Since archaeologists cannot go back in time and directly study prehistoric cultures, they have to find other ways to understand how past cultures might have lived. Sometimes information about present-day cultures (such as the Hopi and Zuni) is helpful because it gives archaeologists clues to questions they should ask about artifacts or rock art. Using ethnography in this way is known as using "ethnographic analogy."

Suggestions of the functional purposes of rock art images are based on ethnographic analogies to ancestral and historic Pueblo agricultural and ceremonial activities. This is done with caution. Practices vary by culture and even within villages of the same culture. It is also common for images to have multiple levels of meaning. For example, a deer-like zoomorph with an apparent archer (as seen on page 33) may, on the surface, appear to be a simple hunting scene. But was it created for hunting instruction, as part of a hunting magic ceremony, to symbolize a tale of supernatural importance, or does the deer-like image represent the spirit-helper of a competing shaman (the archer?) as part of a black magic ceremony? It is also possible that the deer scene is purely symbolic, such as the documented examples of a deer and hunter being used to depict a shaman "shooting" the clouds to bring rain.

As was stated earlier, there are no absolutes in seeking such meanings. However, as David Whitley has stated in Introduction to Rock Art Research, ". . . the archaeological record is in fact a record of human behavior and there is no reason why meaning cannot be derived from archaeological analysis." Some basic similarities may be found after an assessment of multiple lines of independent archaeological evidence to suggest an analogy.

The following are some of the possible *functional categories* for rock art to assist in deriving potential meaning to the images.

CLAN SYMBOLS

Some rock art may be clan or totemic symbols. Clans often have animals or other imagery associated with their people. In describing the function and interpretation of Hopi rock art, it has been suggested that clan symbols show where a clan has been or denotes the location of communal lands. It has also been suggested that such symbols were created during important ritual pilgrimage, either on the route or at a designated location, to mark the successful completion of the pilgrimage. Clan symbols are historically known to represent clan ownership and to denote boundaries. Some hold that clan symbols are direction or location markers since they are found most often near springs, crossings and along trails. It has been noted that animal images are abundant near game trails, canyons and narrow passages where animals could be hunted or ambushed, thus leading to a non-totem interpretation that such images may represent a record of kills, prayers for hunting success, or hunting magic to assist their efforts.

Some clan symbols are abstract in appearance (e.g., an outlined cross for the Sand Clan) and others are stylized (e.g., bear tracks for the Bear Clan). Symbols may also realistically depict subjects for which the clans are named.

Figure 5.1 Possible symbol of the Sand Clan, although this "outlined cross" image is also interpreted as the source of life and sometimes as the planet Venus

Figure 5.2 Possible symbols of the Crane Clan

31

Figure 5.3 Possible symbol of the Lizard Clan

Figure 5.4 Possible symbol of the Bear Clan

Stories and Myths

Rock art is believed to also represent the passing along of tribal myths and stories. These can be either a single image or multiple images. Some multiple images may be linked by a connecting line to show their relationship. The meaning of most of these stories has been lost so that we are limited in simply suggesting that they fit into this category.

Figure 5.5 is similar to other known representations of the Hopi god, Maasaw. Prior to the arrival of the white man, it is said that Maasaw walked among the Hopi and gave them knowledge. He gave them instructions and prophecies. He pointed a path, a way to travel. The depiction may have been a location at which the story of Maasaw was passed on to later generations.

Figure 5.5 Possible representation of Maasaw

In Figure 5.6 there are a number of long-horned animals who appear to be emerging from a crack in the rock face. In some legends, cracks or fissures are thought to connect the underworld to the surface world. These cracks also represent a place of emergence into this world. It has been suggested that such groupings of animals coming out of a fissure represent the story of how game animals emerged into this world. The two anthropomorphs below the animal-like images have "floating orbs" on each side of their heads, suggestive of supernatural powers. One anthropologist suggests that these are the "mother and father of game animals" who escort the animals into this world.

Some images depict everyday events, such as an apparent hunting scene in Figure 5.7, that may be used for instructional purposes or have mythological stories associated with them. As discussed earlier, this scene may be entirely symbolic.

Figure 5.6 Possible game animal Origin story

Figure 5.7 Possible hunting scene, but other interpretations are possible

Figure 5.8 Possible mythical figure

Other images do not appear to resemble any known creature but are human-like or animal-like in appearance. Such images (Figure 5.8) appear to be either imaginary figures or part of a mythological story.

Yavapai rock art can be distinguished from the earlier Archaic and Sinagua rock art based on stylistic differences. The image in Figure 5.9 is a figure on horseback (clearly post-Spanish contact) and is believed to be a representation of Yavapai Akaka, a supernatural being who lived in the rocks and assisted shamans in curing.

The depiction of gods or other supernaturals is believed to be fairly common in rock art. Figure 5.10 shows several figures with multiple feathers. The figures also have "power lines" radiating from their bodies.

Figure 5.9 Possible Yavapai *Akaka* figures on horseback

Figure 5.10 Possible Yavapai figures with feathers and lines of supernatural power from their bodies

FLUTEPLAYER

One of the most recognized images found throughout the Southwest is the image of the **Fluteplayer**. It is found in petroglyphs and pictographs, as well in pottery designs. The classic portrayal of the fluteplayer often includes a hump, a phallus and a flute. In some images, his legs and feet appear to be deformed as though having a club foot. He may also be depicted with a feather, insect antennae or rabbit ears. The figure is sometimes shown with animals, hunters or maidens. In some scenes he is associated with rainmaking. Because of these many traits he has been given a number of functions such as a minstrel, a hunter, a bringer of rain and a fertility figure.

Figure 5.11 Reclining fluteplayer with zoomorph. Note possible rain falling from the fluteplayer's back.

One of the earliest archaeological references to the fluteplayer was by Jesse Fewkes, an ethnographer with the Smithsonian Institution. In 1898 he described a humpbacked Hopi katsina by the name of **Kookopölö**. The term "katsina" refers to the supernatural beings that are believed to visit Hopi villagers during half of the year. Katsinas exercise control over the weather, help in many of the everyday activities of the villagers, punish offenders of ceremonial or social laws and, in general, function as messengers between the spiritual domain and mortals. Katsinas are spiritual messengers.

Figure 5.12 Fluteplayer with possibly a "maiden" suggested by the hair whorls.

Sometime in the 1930s, the term was corrupted as "Kokopelli" when referring to the rock art motif of a flute-playing anthropomorph. Today the "K-word" should only be associated with Southwestern curio shop items, and not with the original Hopi katsina or fluteplayer rock art. The misappropriation of the humpbacked kachina to these images is even more inappropriate in that the Hopi katsina has no flute!

The Hopi never refer to the flute player with the "K-word" but rather with the traditional term for this motif, *Maahu*, or Locust. This may account for the occasional hump back similar to a locust or cicada. Maahu is an ancient deity, perhaps predating the katsina religion that is involved in the Hopi stories of emergence into this world. According to Hopi belief, the depicted fluteplayer represents a locust that when heard, is thought to be fluting to bring about warm weather conditions necessary for planting. The rather prodigious mating habits of the locust are the most likely source for associating fertility with the fluteplayer.

It is not know exactly where in the Four Corners area the standing, humpless and non-phallic fluteplayer figure originated. The figure begins to emerge about A.D. 800. It is this image that has misappropriated the name Kookopölö to achieve a high level of public awareness in tourist art (perhaps because of the non-sexual aspects of this image). Some archaeologists have suggested that some of these early fluteplayer images may represent a **puchteca**, an Aztec or Toltec trader from Central Mexico. In this interpretation, the "hump" is actually a basket with trade goods.

A very fascinating discussion of the origins of the Kokopelli phenomenon can be found in *Kokopelli: The Making of an Icon* by Ekkehart Malotki, a professor emeritus at Northern Arizona University.

SKYWATCHING

The science of archaeoastronomy is a relatively new branch of archaeology. It seeks to study how different cultures have dealt with the balance of terrestrial and cosmological events. The

Figure 5.13 Standing Fluteplayer petroglyph but without the hump or other typical features.

archaeoastronomer is largely concerned with the cosmologies, myths, calendar systems, navigation and other celestial phenomena marked by prehistoric cultures. The use of rock art in such systems is a common starting point.

Figure 5.14 Mosaic of various petroglyphs and pictographs that have possible astronomical meanings

Several rock art symbols are sought by archaeoastronomers, who then attempt to determine whether any celestial phenomenon can be attached to its creation. The term motif can be used in this context. A motif in rock art signifies a major theme, figure or design used repeatedly. A grouping of such motifs is presented in Figure 5.14. Among these are concentric circles, found throughout the Southwest that is said to represent "Father Sun." The image can be found with one, two or three circles around a central dot. The circles are said to report the emanating power of the sun, while the dot represents the Sun Father's umbilicus, or power center.

An outlined-cross is associated with several meanings, one of which is the Morning or Evening Star (Venus). Asterisks and crosses have also been suggested from time to time to represent a star or the sun. The circular images with protruding lines can also represent the sun.

These images may have been created to mark an historical event, such as a comet or eclipse. Others may represent a calendar timing event, such as the first appearance of the Morning Star (Venus) associated with some ceremony or planting. Some, as found at the V Bar V

Figure 5.15 Equinox sun/shadow petroglyph at V Bar V

Heritage Site, are used in conjunction with sun and shadow effects to mark the passing of the sun at equinoxes. As shown in Figure 5.15, the images are placed to be tangent to a shaft of sun to mark its passage at a specific time of year. But a word of caution is needed here again! Not all circle-dots, or concentric circles, have celestial meaning. Detailed calculations and seasonal observations are needed to confirm such a purpose.

Sometimes, as with the passing down of stories or myths, a celestial depiction is made as a reminder or for instructional purposes for those who were charged with watching the sun, moon and stars to determine the appropriate time for planting, ceremonies and rituals. A pictograph at the Palatki Heritage Site (Figure 5.16) appears to depict the positions of the sun on the opposite horizon at the time of the solstices and equinoxes. The image resembles a mirror-image of the opposite canyon horizon topography. The round image is in the position of sunrise on the horizon at the summer solstice, while the double black triangles mark the sun's position at the two equinoxes. The last black triangle is in the position of the winter solstice sunrise.

Figure 5.16 Pictograph of possible seasonal horizon markers at Palatki

Sex and Gender

Southwestern rock art is known to contain depictions of human sexuality and gender symbols. The preponderance of anthropomorphic figures in the Sedona area does not have sufficient detail to determine the sex of the image. Those that do, however, are predominantly male (Figure 5.17). Anthropomorphs with female genitalia or breasts are rare but figures with the elaborate or *butterfly whorls* hairstyle, as seen in the earlier image with a fluteplayer, are usually interpreted as female. This distinctive tribal hairstyle for women was worn by Hopi maidens. To make this hairdo, a young woman's mother would wind her hair around a curved piece of wood to give it a round shape, then remove the wood frame. Historically, only unmarried young women wore this complex hairstyle.

Figure 5.17 Petroglyph of a male anthropomorph

The *matrilineal* structure of Pueblo society was recognized as early as the 1880s by archaeologists who accompanied the first railroad builders into Arizona and New Mexico. This means that clan affiliation is determined through the female line, and children "belong" to the mother's clan. They are also *matrilocal*, meaning that husbands traditionally move into the bride's family household. Their society is matriarchal, meaning that homes and farm land are owned by and inherited from the mother, and a wife has the right to divorce and evict her husband. Although Pueblo societies in prehistoric times were probably matriarchal, farming, hunting, war, ceremonial pursuits and duties were associated with men. Therefore, it would not be surprising that most rock art anthropomorphs are male.

Figure 5.18 Petroglyph of mating zoomorphs

Few archaeologists have studied rock art that depicts sex, reproduction, or gender in depth. One of the books on this subject is *Ambiguous Images: Gender and Rock Art* by Kelley A. Hays-Gilpin, an associate professor at Northern Arizona University.

SHAMANISM

Most cultures throughout history have shown an abiding fascination with magic and supernaturalism. The recorded stories of the historic pueblo communities amply demonstrate that this fascination extends to Southwestern cultures and most likely to their ancestral cultures. Magic and supernaturalism were the tools of a **shaman**. A Shaman could cure ailments, but also cause them. They were respected but also feared. The shaman was the religious mediator between the natural and the supernatural. It was believed that the shaman had the power to travel into the spiritual world. There, the shaman could escort the dead, retrieve lost souls, even converse with spirits from the past - animal spirits or spirits of ancient shamen - and then bring back messages of wisdom.

Shamans often began such a spiritual voyage by going into a trance or altered state of consciousness. During a trance, people believe, the soul of the shaman departs from his body, either to ascend into the sky or to descend into the underworld. A trance could be induced by chanting, beating a drum, fasting, retreating into isolation, or eating hallucinogenic substances. Such trances typically produced trance imagery that may account for some rock art imagery.

The depiction of a shaman in rock art is often identified by exaggerated fingers and/or toes since these were considered power centers of the body.

Figure 5.19 Petroglyph of possible shaman

Alexander Stephen noted in his *Hopi Journal* of 1892 that he observed a ceremony involving the sprinkling of corn meal with the left hand. He reported that the left hand was regarded as sacred. It was used to place and remove ceremonial masks, and to place prayer-sticks, feathers and meal offerings. The right hand was used to carry food to the mouth so was regarded as ceremonially defiled. Stephen reported that during a Hopi "discharming rite" or exorcism the left moccasin was removed. Figure 5.19 has the left foot (toes) exposed while the toes are not visible on the right foot. Zuni reportedly have a similar exorcism ceremony involving the left foot. This comparison is intriguing but by no means defining.

As with most rock art the suggested interpretations or functions that have been discussed are speculative. These anthropomorphs could equally be identified as deities, specific supernatural beings, dead ancestors, spirit figures or totems.

Figure 5.20 Pictograph of possible shaman

6
ROCK ART PANELS

Up to this point, rock art images have been presented as individual elements. This is seldom the case in the field. Most rock art is found in groupings of images. Some groupings contain a small number while others can number in the dozens. The selection of the location for rock art imagery appears to have been carefully planned. While some rock art is found at or near habitation sites, many panels are found at remote locations, far from significant habitation sites. Landscape research is a relatively new concept in rock art studies. These studies attempt to establish a relationship of rock art sites to immediate or nearby geologic features, including the rock art panel. The concept is that since these cultures were intimately in tune with the earth, the location of rock art was as symbolic as the rock art images themselves.

As was discussed earlier, attempts to attach meaning to rock images require that they be examined within the context of the culture that created them. It is equally important to examine them within the context of place. The chosen location of rock art can provide clues to their possible meaning. Some have suggested that they were created at isolated ceremonial centers or as ceremonial shrines used during annual pilgrimages. Finding images of corn near fields has suggested the use of magic to induce good crops. Similarly, the large number of game animal and hunter images found along or near game trails has suggested the use of hunting magic. It was thought that the underworld could be reached through caves, rock shelters and other openings in the rock, so these locations often contain rock art.

Studies of Puebloan cultures have shown that while rock art symbols have the power to evoke narrative traditions, they can also enhance the significance of places. Murals are sometimes found in kivas (ceremonial rooms). Painted scenes of katsina and supernatural birds and animals probably depict supplications for rain or fertility to crops.

Another interesting area of landscape research attempts to relate the placement of some rock art sites to acoustic properties. It has been noted that some sites that have ceremonial suggestions also have the ability to enhance rituals where chanting, singing or drumming may have played a role. Echo intensity has been digitally measured at regular intervals along some canyons and it was found that the intensity spiked only at rock art locations. These studies suggest that these acoustically enhanced locations may have been public ceremonial sites rather than sites for private rituals. Correlating prehistoric rock art with echoing locations suggest that sound may have been a motivation some rock art locations since cultural significance of echoes has been shown through myths that attribute echoes to spirits. Some of the sites that have been tested and have been shown to have these echo sound qualities include Honanki, Red Canyon (Palatki), Red Tank Draw's canyon, Red Tank Draw's boulder by the road, and Montezuma Castle.

Below are several rock art panels. See if you can distinguish the individual images and categorize them as anthropomorphs, zoomorphs, geometrics, etc. As you review these panels, remember that as stated earlier, the cultures responsible for the rock art have been gone for hundreds or thousands of years. Little is known of their beliefs, myths, rituals or world view. We cannot debrief the creators for answers to our burning questions. The placing of rock art images into functional categories, as done in the previous chapter, is an attempt to bridge this knowledge gap with ethnographic analogy. However, the over-riding question remains -- to what extent can we use historic ethnographic information from Pueblo Indians to interpret the much older rock art? The bad news answer is – we will never know. The good news answer is – by using available ethnographic information we can potentially touch the minds of these people and appreciate the complexity of their life struggle and the intelligence they brought to bear for their survival.

Figure 6.1 This pictograph panel has negative handprints, various zoomorphs, lines of dots as well as a white and red series of diamond shapes. There also appears to be a row of anthropomorphs. Note how many of the images are faded to different degrees. This may provide some clues as to their relative ages.

Figure 6.2 This petroglyph panel has zoomorphs, spirals, circled dots, an outlined cross, as well as anthropomorphs. Note the white blotch. This is the result of a vandal applying plaster to the image in an unsuccessful attempt to take an impression of a petroglyph. As can be seen, the plaster residue does not wash off, damaging the image for all future visitors. Vandalism is a greater threat to these heritage treasures than environmental factors.

Figure 6.3 This petroglyph panel shows a herd of zoomorphs, an anthropomorph, a spiral and various geometric designs.

Figure 6.4 This boulder, along a prehistoric trail, has multiple geometric petroglyphs

Figure 6.5 This pictograph panel has geometric designs, outlined crosses, zoomorphs, anthropomorphs and geometric designs.

7
DIGITAL ROCK ART ENHANCEMENT

The images captured in this book are among the clearest and best preserved. Petroglyphs generally are better preserved, because they do not fade with exposure to the natural elements of sun, wind, and rain. They will soften and darken as the desert varnish gradually reclaims the cleared area, but they are still visible unless covered by lichen. Pictographs, however, are much more fragile. Direct sunlight will fade them quickly. Unless protected under an overhang, rain and wind will also have a detrimental effect.

Fortunately, digital technology tools are being developed to help recover some of these faded pictographs and even reveal hidden elements with some petroglyphs. New tools are available that can enhance digital photographs to bring out faint pictographs that are invisible or barely visible to the naked eye. Adobe Photoshop™ allows for alternative color spaces. Each color channel can be displayed and manipulated. In some cases images that were nearly invisible can be brought out in alternative enhanced colors. A freeware photo enhancement software package called ImageJ can also be used. Jon Harman, Ph.D., has developed a plug-in tool for ImageJ that I have used with success. Here is how Dr. Harman describes the process:

> *"The technique consists of applying a Karhunen-Loeve transform to the colors of the image. This diagonalizes the covariance (or optionally the correlation) matrix of the colors. Next the contrast for each color is stretched to equalize the color variances. At this point the colors are uncorrelated and fill the colorspace. Finally the inverse transform is used to map the colors back to an approximation of the original. Other names for related techniques are Principal Components Analysis and Hotelling transformation. The decorrelation stretch calculation produces a 3x3 matrix that is then applied to the colors in the image."*

Now I get it! Not really. All I know is that it works very well and was used to produce the enhanced images that follow.

The discovery of some previously unseen, or incompletely seen, images is causing some archaeologists to consider photographing many previously recorded sites with digital technology. Who knows what we may find?

Figure 7.1 The enhanced petroglyph panel reveals that the surface was first abraded to provide a smoother working surface. It also clearly shows the "power lines" emanating from the bodies of these Yavapai figures.

Figure 7.2 In this pictograph, the colors are enhanced to bring out any hidden or faded white images. This shows that the "erased" shield to the left had many of the same characteristics of the shield to its right. It also shows that the center shield has "images" in at least three of the four quadrants that are barely visible without the enhancement.

Fig. 7.3 This color enhancement reveals many barely visible images and enhances others. A herd of black zoomorphs are more clearly defined below the white snake. The lower left image is now even more intriguing with the enhanced yellow imagery.

8
VISITING ROCK ART SITES

Rock art sites are an important part of America's cultural heritage. They should be preserved and protected for continual study and for future generations to view and appreciate. We are rapidly losing these rock art sites due to senseless vandalism, but also just to natural erosion and decomposition due to lichen growth. The deterioration and eventual loss of rock art is inevitable

To discourage anyone who might be inclined to deface prehistoric rock art sites, these archaeological resources are protected by federal, state and local laws. Severe fines and prison time can result for each offense. Arizona's State Historical Preservation Office (azstateparks.com/volunteer/v_sitestewards.html) has a statewide system of over 900 volunteer site stewards who patrol many of the less visited sites. The site stewards report vandalism that they find in progress, or after the fact. They have been trained in evidence preservation until law enforcement arrives on the scene. If you are a resident of Arizona and would like to help with this invaluable service, visit their website for more information.

Beside the Verde Valley Archaeology Center (www.verdevalleyarchaeology.org), other local volunteer organizations, such as the Friends of the Forest Sedona (www.friendsoftheforestsedona.org) and the Verde Valley Chapter of the Arizona Archaeological Society (www.azarchsoc.org) also have cultural resource protection programs. Check in your area on how you can get involved.

Unfortunately, due to potential vandalism, many rock art sites are not made public. In some rock art books, the names of locations are actually changed or made-up to help hide the site. Fortunately, there are several sites that are easily accessible in the Sedona/Verde Valley area. These are:

Palatki/Red Cliffs Heritage Site
This U.S. Forest Service site features a cliff dwelling, plus several areas of pictograph rock art.

Honanki Heritage Site
This U.S. Forest Service site is west of the Palatki Heritage Site and reached over an unimproved road that can be rather difficult depending upon weather conditions. It features a very large cliff dwelling. It is thought that this was one of the largest dwelling complexes in the area, containing up to 75 rooms. There are several areas of pictograph rock art.

V Bar V Heritage Site
This U.S. Forest Service site, on a historic cattle ranch, features the largest petroglyph site in the Verde Valley with over 1,030 images. The site has no pictographs.

Red Tank Draw
This site is accessed via unimproved Forest Service roads, limited to high-clearance vehicles. Some jeep tours have permits to take groups to this site.

Bell Trail
This Forest Service trail is southeast of Sedona near Beaver Creek. It has several rock art boulders with petroglyphs and cupules starting about 1.8 miles into the trail.

When visiting these or other sites, please observe the following common sense rules:

- Be sensitive to the site's spiritual importance. Some sites are still visited by Native Americans for religious purposes.

- If a trail exists, please stay on it. Not only might there be hidden snakes, cactus and other dangers, but you may be treading on important artifacts or unseen elements underfoot.

- Do not alter, move or remove anything in the area. These may be clues to the origin and dating of the rock art.

- Never "highlight" rock art to try to better see the images. Any material added to the rock art can be potentially damaging.

- Never clean rock art. This is a job for professional conservators who are specialists in rock art care.

- Only view, sketch or photograph rock art. Attempts to trace or make molds of rock art have been shown to damage these fragile surfaces.

- Add nothing to the site. Adding things like rock shrines is disrespectful to the Native Americans who may still hold the site as spiritually important.

- Never touch rock art. Touching can smudge and disintegrate delicate pictograph paint layers. Oils, salts and acids on fingers can hasten both pictograph and petroglyph destruction.

- Camp away – never build a fire near rock art. Heat can damage painted surfaces and potentially add soot over rock surfaces.

Enjoy your visits. Please help us preserve these cultural heritage sites for future generations.

SUGGESTED READING

Cole, Sally J. 1990. *Legacy on Stone.* Johnson Books, Boulder, CO
    The book surveys the cultural history and rock art traditions of the Colorado Plateau and the Four Corners region from archaic hunters and gatherers to the Anasazi, Fremont, Navajo and Ute peoples.

Hays-Gilpin, Kelley A. 2004. *Ambiguous Images: Gender and Rock Art.* Alta Mira Press, Walnut Creek, CA
    This book reviews rock art throughout the world to show how rock art informs us about prehistoric gender and social life.

Malotki, Ekkehart. 2007. *The Rock Art of Arizona: Art for Life's Sake.* Kiva Publishing, Walnut, CA
    With a foreword by Governor Janet Napolitano this book contains 380 color photographs, over 130 drawings, and numerous charts and maps. In addition to describing the various rock art styles and traditions, the author provides insights into what may have compelled Arizona's ancestral artists to produce the rock art.

Malotki, Ekkehart. 2000. *Kokopelli: The Making of an Icon.* University of Nebraska Press, Lincoln, NE
    Kokopelli is a very erroneously applied to the fluteplayer motif in the rock art of the American Southwest. This book traces the origins of this icon in popular culture and suggests that "the K-Word" has no place in legitimate rock art research.

Schaafsma, Polly. 1980. *Indian Rock Art of the Southwest.* University of New Mexico Press, Albuquerque.
    Still a classic covering rock art across the American Southwest.

Whitley, David S. 2005. *Introduction to Rock Art Research.* Left Coast Press, Walnut Creek, CA
    A good general overview of the processes needed to document, interpret and preserve rock art.

Zoll, Kenneth J. 2008. *Sinagua Sunwatchers: An Archaeoastronomy Survey of the Sacred Mountain Basin.* VVAC Press, Camp Verde
    This monograph provides an introduction to archaeoastronomy as well as documenting the solar calendar at the V Bar V Heritage site and surrounding area astronomical features.

Zoll, Kenneth J. 2014. *Ancient Astronomy of Central Arizona.* VVAC Press, Camp Verde
    This book describes several solar calendar discoveries in Central Arizona that employ rock art.

CPSIA information can be obtained
at www.ICGtesting.com
Printed in the USA
LVHW072008220819
628593LV00024B/410/P